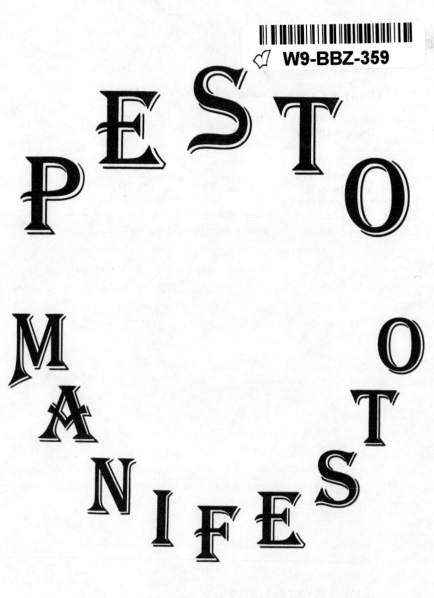

PESTO MANIFESTO

LOREL NAZZARO

CHICAGO REVIEW PRESS

Library of Congress Cataloging-in-Publication Data

Nazzaro, Lorel.
  Pesto manifesto.

  Includes index.
  1. Pestos. I. Title.
TX819.P45N38   1988   641.8'14   88-2577
ISBN 1-55652-028-X

Copyright © 1988 by Lorel Nazzaro
All rights reserved
Printed in the United States of America
First edition
Published by Chicago Review Press Incorporated,
814 N. Franklin St., Chicago, IL 60610
ISBN: 1-55652-028-X

In memory of my
warm and happy Neopolitan father,
Landis A. Nazzaro

CONTENTS

ACKNOWLEDGMENTS

I wish to thank my friends Linda Rosen and Jean Beal for their research, my husband Jack for his inspired suggestions and assistance with the word processor, my sister-in-law Anne Beuttas for her "pesto passion," and my daughter Isabel for her energizing love.

With basil then I will begin—
whose scent is wondrous pleasing.

—Michael Drayton, "Polyolbion"
English poet, 1563–1631

INTRODUCTION

PESTO PRINCIPLES

Pesto is a sauce made from fresh basil, garlic, grated Parmesan cheese, olive oil, and pine nuts. It is of Italian origin and the word *pesto* means pounded, as traditionally it was made by grinding the ingredients together by hand in a mortar and pestle.

Its prime ingredient, basil, has a great affinity with tomatoes and, like garlic, leads to passionate addiction. Its pungent flavor has made pesto one of the most popular and up-and-coming foods in the country. The versatility of this "upscale catsup" is limited only by your imagination. It's also nutritious. Olive oil and garlic are cholesterol killers; cheese and nuts are a good source of protein.

Basil is known as the "King of Herbs." In Ancient Greece, the king was the only one deemed worthy to mark the start of the harvest by the first cutting with a golden sickle.

In Eastern cultures basil plays an important role in religious and spiritual traditions. In India it is considered a passport to paradise where it is said every good Hindu goes to bed with a basil leaf on his breast. Because of its cleansing effect on malarious air, it is thought of as the protecting spirit of Hindu households.

Persian and Egyptian women traditionally plant basil on graves of loved ones, and in Israel Jews carry basil sprays on their breasts during religious feasts. The intense aroma or "shock of pleasure" (as Eleanor Perényi describes it in *Green Thoughts*) given off by basil cuttings has been credited for the reverence people have given it. Today, at Caswell and Massey Apothecaries in New York, one can purchase an oil of basil for a princely $18.50 per half ounce.

Basil thrives in warm weather and full sun. It can be started indoors in the spring and transplanted outside once its second pair of true leaves develop. These seedlings must be placed in soil at least 70 degrees warm (otherwise the plant's growth is set back, causing it to become spindley and never reaching true maturity).

Because we have cold springs in Maine, I direct seed sweet basil (*Ocimum Basilicum*) outdoors in late May. My garden is on an open southern slope and provides basil with its necessities for growth—full sun, rich soil, and good drainage. Germination takes 10 to 14 days. (It seems like an eternity.) But finally I spot the sturdy little seedlings thrusting through the soil. Meticulous weeding and lots of encouragement (I speak to my plants in Italian) are very important.

My garden is organic. When the snows melt in April, I drive to the local fish market in my truck to pick up fish guts. They are worked into my compost pile, a collection of uneaten foods and vegetable peelings that when broken down in form and chemistry will give new life to the soil. I water the pile and cover it tightly with large plastic sheets. Once a week I uncover and toss it until late June

4

when it has turned into rich brown soil and is applied as a side dressing to boost the growth of my established plants.

By early July I can start to make "early pesto" with thinnings. Because these plants are young and tender, it is mild in flavor but satisfies a pesto lover's craving. The thinning process also aerates the soil nicely. Pinching off the tops of young plants causes them to branch out and grow strong and bushy. Basil is easily damaged by frost. Late harvest basil will survive a mild frost if watered with a fine spray and covered securely with a plastic tarp.

In the fall I go on a search for "mysterious piles" (manure for fertilizer). I call on my friend who raises rabbits, another friend who keeps dairy cows, and clean my chicken house of its rich droppings from our organically raised hens. This may be taking an extreme statement to its extreme, but in our culture of toxic waste and disposable commodities, it feels good to put good things into the earth.

After rototilling the manure into the harvested garden, I plant a cover crop of winter rye. Rows between the beds are lined with seaweed.

Basil is a shallow rooted plant and will grow indoors in clay pots. It needs sun, rich soil, and plant food. Many seed stores carry an organic variety based on seaweed emulsion. *Ocimum Minimum* or "pot basil" is a smaller and neater variety which some people prefer.

In 1962 a Dark Purple or Opal Basil was bred

at the University of Connecticut. It has the unique distinction of being the only herb ever awarded the All-American Medal. Although I prefer using the standard green leafed sweet basil for making pesto, the purple is unusual and a sprig makes an attractive plate ornament.

Most large grocery stores carry fresh basil when it is in season. Usually sold in small bundles, it can be found in the refrigerated fresh produce section. It won't be organically grown. For that you will need to inquire at a health or specialty foods store. I know of several Italian markets that carry fresh basil year round—it comes from the Carolinas or California—but it's not organically grown. I prefer organically grown produce because it is free of chemical fertilizers and simply tastes much better.

Always use fresh basil when making pesto. I know of a recipe that calls for dried basil and fresh spinach but I do not recommend it. This "pesto imposter" lacks the true flavor and aroma of real pesto.

If you wish to buy pesto I would again suggest health or specialty foods stores for buying it fresh in season or fresh-frozen off season. I have seen jars of canned pesto on the shelves of Italian and imported foods stores year round. It comes from Italy, and although it is tasty, it lacks the bite or "zing" of fresh pesto.

Pesto is an excellent food for backpacking. I usually bring a frozen container along with some pasta for a satisfying and nutritious meal. Even thawed, pesto will keep unrefrigerated for several days.

Basil flourishes in the warm, sunny climate of Italy and has found its way into Italian cuisine more so than in any other country. "See Naples and die" is an old Italian proverb. I say "Eat pesto and live," but not without trying some of my recipes. *Pesto Manifesto* means to inspire you. Enjoy!

—Lorel Nazzaro

PESTO POWER

 ## THE RECIPE

Makes 12 ounces

In a blender or food processor mix at high speed:

> *3 cups firmly packed fresh basil leaves*
> *2 large cloves of garlic*
> *2 tablespoons grated Parmesan cheese*
> *⅞ cup olive oil*

Blend thoroughly and add

> *½ cup pine nuts*

Blend for 10 seconds more.

This is a basic traditional recipe for pesto. I prefer to use a small amount of cheese in the preparation. Most dishes do not lend themselves to a lot of cheese; but some are enhanced by the addition of freshly grated cheese at serving time.

Pesto can be stored in the refrigerator for at least four weeks. It also freezes well (particularly when made with a small amount of cheese) in small plastic containers. It may be stored frozen for up to a year.

When pesto is exposed to air, a natural enzymatic action will cause it to darken. This discoloration does not in any way indicate spoilage.

APPETIZERS

&

SNACKS

PESTO GUACAMOLE

Makes 2 cups

In blender, blend:

1 tablespoon pesto
1 cup sour cream
1 avocado
1 tablespoon lemon juice
1 tomato, diced

Add:
Salt and pepper to taste. Serve with taco chips.

PESTO QUICK DIP FOR CHIPS

Makes 2 cups

Mix well:

8 ounces sour cream
8 ounces cottage cheese
1 tablespoon pesto
1 teaspoon Dijon or whole-grain mustard
3–4 drops Worcestershire

13

TOFU STICKS

Slice firm tofu into ½-inch-thick strips. Sprinkle with soy sauce, and marinate for 1 hour in pesto. Roll sticks in Italian bread crumbs. Quickly brown in hot olive oil. Remove and let sit on paper towel.

PESTO PÂTÉ

Makes 2½ cups

This is a good appetizer when vegetarians come for dinner.

In a blender, blend:

1 cup cream cheese
1 cup chopped walnuts
4 ounces pesto
Dash of salt

Chill for 3 hours.

THE RITZY PESTO

This is a "late night munchies" desperation invention. The people I give this recipe to think I'm crazy—until they try it.

Spread Ritz crackers with crunchy peanut butter. Top with a little catsup and a dollop of pesto. Garnish with a slice of red onion.

 ## PESTO POPCORN

This beats all those other flavored popcorns you've ever tried!

Toss freshly popped popcorn with a mixture of equal parts melted butter and pesto. Sprinkle with extra pine nuts and grated cheese (I like to use Parmesan or Romano).

PESTO BAGEL CHIPS

Spread soft brie cheese on these, and they will taste especially good.

Toss thinly sliced pieces of bagel with pesto. Roast in 350°F oven until crisp. Place on paper towel, salt lightly, and store in airtight containers.

 # PESTOED EGGS

Slice hard boiled eggs in half and mash each yolk with:

1 teaspoon mayonnaise
1 teaspoon pesto
½ teaspoon Dijon mustard

Refill egg whites with this mixture and top with capers and freshly ground pepper.

SMOKED MUSSELS IN PESTO

This is an elegant but simple hot appetizer.

Gently toss smoked mussels in pesto. Serve over cooked, buttered "nests" of fine angel hair pasta.

ESCARGOT IN PESTO

As a Christmas gift I received a can of California escargot packed in water. It was a natural "pesto match."

Simply drain the can and gently sauté them in pesto. I serve them with rounds of rye toast crackers.

SOFT SHELLED CRABS IN PESTO

You may want to try adding a squeeze of lemon and a small dollop of horseradish to the pesto.

Gently sauté crabs in butter until done (approximately three minutes each side). Pour pesto over crabs (one tablespoon per crab). Toss gently and simmer for one minute.

PESTO SPINACH BALLS

Makes 24 appetizers

You can make these ahead of time and keep them handy in the freezer.

2 10-ounce packages frozen spinach—cooked,
drained, and chopped
2 cups seasoned croutons
1 cup grated Parmesan cheese
4 eggs, lightly beaten
4 tablespoons melted butter
4 tablespoons pesto
Dash of nutmeg

Blend all ingredients in a blender. Shape into balls and place on a cookie sheet lined with waxed paper. Freeze for 1 hour. Place balls in airtight container or Ziplock plastic bag. Store frozen until ready to cook. Preheat oven to 375°F. Bake balls on ungreased cookie sheet 10–15 minutes.

PESTO-OLIVE-CHEESE NUGGETS

Makes 24 appetizers

24 large stuffed green olives
1 cup grated sharp cheddar cheese
2 tablespoons softened butter
2 tablespoons pesto
¾ cup flour
½ teaspoon paprika

Thoroughly blend together cheese, butter, and pesto. Mix in flour and paprika, using your hands to form into dough. Form dough around olives in a thin layer. Place on ungreased cookie sheet and bake at 400°F until dough is golden in color, about 15 minutes.

BAKED GOAT'S CHEESE

Gently toss cubes of goat's cheese (boucheron or chevre are nice) in pesto. Wrap in large spinach leaves and bake until cheese is soft and leaves are wilted. Serve with a side garnish of smoked scallops.

PESTO CRESCENT ROLL PIZZA DELIGHT

Makes 42 2-inch pieces

Keep this in the refrigerator for a healthy snack.

*2 8-ounce packages of refrigerated
crescent rolls
8 ounces sour cream or whipped cream cheese
(or 4 ounces of each)
2 tablespoons pesto
3–4 cups diced fresh broccoli, cauliflower,
mushrooms, and tomatoes.*

Separate dough into 4 long rectangles. Place crosswise in ungreased 12″ × 15″ pan. Press edges up 1 inch to form sides. Seal perforations. Bake 15 minutes at 375°F. Combine sour cream and/or cream cheese with pesto. Spread over cooked "rolls" crust. Top with vegetables. Season with salt, pepper, garlic powder, and dried oregano.

DEEP FRIED BRIE

Makes 10–12 appetizers

Cut ½–¾ pound of Brie into small shapes. Do
not peel. Beat 1 egg with 1 tablespoon pesto.
Dip cheese pieces first into flour, then egg
mixture, then bread crumbs. Chill for 1 hour.
Cook in hot oil for 10–15 seconds until
browned on the outside and melted within.

PESTO BRIE PIE

Slice a round of Brie in half crosswise. Spread
with pesto (on bottom layer) and top with other
half. Gently warm in oven at 300°F for a few
minutes. Slice in wedges. This goes nicely with
rice cakes.

PESTO-VEGETABLE JUICE

In a juicer combine fresh carrot, celery, and
tomato that have been chopped. For every eight
ounces of juice add 1 teaspoon pesto, a dash of
Worcestershire, and a tiny dollop of
horseradish. Process in juicer and add salt and
pepper to taste. Add some vodka for a great
Bloody Mary.

SQUASH BLOSSOMS WITH PESTO

Pick 6 large squash blossoms.
  Batter consists of:

¾ cup cornstarch
¼ cup flour
1 teaspoon baking powder
½ teaspoon pepper
1 teaspoon grated Parmesan or Romano cheese
⅔ cup beer or water
1 egg
Olive oil

In a bowl mix together first five ingredients of
batter. Add beer or water and egg. Stir until
smooth. Pour olive oil in large skillet to depth
of ½ inch. Heat over medium heat. Dip
blossoms into batter and fry 2–3 minutes,
turning once until golden brown and crisp.
Place blossoms on a cookie sheet lined with a
paper towel. Drizzle tops with a little pesto and
pop in hot oven (preheated at 400°F) for three
minutes to make them super crispy. Serve with
soy sauce for dipping.

SOUPS

POTAGE SAINT GERMAIN

Serves 3–4

A good early summer soup. It's OK to use
lettuce that has started to bolt.

4 ounces pesto
1 small head lettuce
1½ pounds cooked peas
3 cups chicken broth
2 teaspoons salt
1 teaspoon sugar
Black pepper
Watercress

In a large pan gently warm the pesto and briefly
cook the lettuce and peas in it. Put lettuce and
peas in blender with salt, sugar, and 1 cup
chicken broth. Blend until smooth. Put this
mixture back into the pan with the rest of the
chicken broth. Bring to a quick boil. Serve
topped with freshly ground black pepper and
sprigs of watercress.

SQUASH BISQUE

Serves 6–8

2 pounds peeled winter squash
1 pound ripe tomatoes, peeled
¼ cup barley
4 ounces pesto
2 tablespoons chopped scallions
Sprinkle of allspice
2 quarts rich beef stock
2 tablespoons cooking sherry
2 slices bacon, fried crisp and crumbled
2 tablespoons chopped parsley

Chop squash and tomatoes. Place them in a large pot with all ingredients except sherry, bacon, and parsley. Cover and simmer over medium heat for one hour, stirring often. If desired whirl in blender until smooth. Season with salt and pepper and add sherry. Serve topped with bacon and parsley. Pesto Croutons offered on the side go nicely. (See Index.)

PESTO POTATO CHOWDER

Serves 6–8

This is very nice served with Pesto Popovers. (See Index.)

¼ pound salt pork, diced
1 cup coarsely chopped onion
½ cup chopped celery
4 ounces pesto
3 cups diced raw potatoes
¼ cup finely chopped carrot
4 cups milk
1 cup water
2 cups canned cream-style corn
1 cup shredded cheddar cheese

In a soup kettle fry salt pork until crisp. Add onion and celery and cook until soft. Add pesto, potatoes, and carrot. Cook 10 minutes, stirring occasionally. Add milk and water. Mix thoroughly. Cover and simmer for 15 minutes. Stir in corn and cheese. Season to taste and simmer uncovered for about 5 minutes.

CREAMY MINESTRONE
WITH PESTO

Serves 4–6

2 tablespoons minced onion
½ cup minced celery
2 teaspoons olive oil
2 turnips and tops, all minced
½ cup shredded cabbage
½ cup chopped beet greens or Swiss chard
¼ cup minced parsley
3 cups rich veal or chicken stock
2 cups half and half cream
4 ounces pesto
Grated Parmesan cheese

Sauté onion and celery in oil until soft. Add vegetables, parsley, and stock. Cover, bring to a boil, and simmer for 20 minutes. Add cream, reheat, and salt and pepper to taste. At serving time, drizzle warm pesto over the top and pass the Parmesan cheese.

LENTIL SOUP

Serves 4–6

1 tablespoon oil
1 cup chopped onion
2 cups dried lentils
2 quarts water
2 potatoes, cooked, peeled, and diced
1 large carrot, grated
2 tablespoons pesto
2 cups tomato juice
¾ cup shredded spinach
½ cup dry white wine
Salt and pepper
Goat's cheese

Heat oil in heavy kettle and sauté onion until transparent. Add lentils and water. Bring to a boil, cover, and simmer until lentils are tender—about 2 hours. Replenish water if necessary to keep lentils covered. Add potatoes, carrot, pesto, tomato juice, and spinach. Cook 5 minutes more and stir in wine. Salt and pepper to taste. Serve with crumbled goat's cheese.

TOMATO SOUP WITH DUMPLINGS

Serves 4
with 2 dumplings each

1 tablespoon butter
1 onion, chopped
1 stalk celery, chopped
1 carrot, chopped
1 tablespoon flour
4 cups chicken broth
4 large tomatoes, chopped
2 tablespoons pesto
Splash of cognac
Salt and pepper

Heat butter and sauté onion, celery, and carrot for 4 minutes. Stir in flour and add broth, stirring with a whisk. Add tomatoes and pesto. Simmer uncovered for 20 minutes. Puree in a blender. Return to pot with cognac and seasonings. When dumplings are ready, reheat soup and cook them gently in it.

DUMPLINGS

½ pound spinach, cooked, drained, and
chopped
½ cup grated Parmesan cheese
1 cup ricotta cheese
1 teaspoon salt
1 egg
Mixture of ½ tablespoon melted butter and ½
tablespoon pesto
½ cup flour

Mix spinach with cheeses, salt, egg, and half
the butter-pesto mixture. Refrigerate for 1 hour.
Shape dough into balls, roll in flour, and drop a
few at a time into gently boiling soup. When
they rise to the surface, remove with a slotted
spoon and place on a buttered baking pan.
Preheat broiler. Sprinkle the dumplings with a
little more grated Parmesan cheese, drizzle with
remaining pesto-butter, and broil until cheese
browns.

SOUPE DE POISSON
AND PESTO

Serves 4

This is the best fish soup I've ever tasted.

2 tablespoons olive oil
¼ cup chopped onion
½ cup chopped green pepper
½ cup chopped leeks
½ cup chopped carrots
1 hot red pepper, crumbled
1 bay leaf
½ teaspoon dried thyme
1 cup dry white wine
1 cup chopped tomatoes
⅓ pound potatoes
1 cup water
1 pound codfish
½ pint scallops
2 tablespoons pesto
1 cup heavy cream
¼ cup chopped parsley
Salt and pepper

Heat oil in a kettle and add onion, green pepper, leeks, and carrots. Cook until onion wilts. Add red pepper, bay leaf, thyme, wine, and tomatoes. Add peeled and chopped potatoes. Cover and cook 10 minutes. Add water, uncover, and cook 5 minutes. Add fish and scallops. Simmer 3 minutes. Swirl in pesto and cream. Bring to a quick boil. Top with parsley and season to taste.

EASY BORSCHT WITH PESTO TOPPING

Serves 6

1 pound beef brisket or meaty short ribs, cut up
1 cup chopped onion
1 bay leaf
1 teaspoon salt
1 teaspoon pepper
6 cups water
3 tablespoons pesto
3 cups grated beets
1 cup grated carrot
1 cup diced potato
1 8-ounce can tomato puree
3 cups shredded cabbage
16 ounces sour cream or yogurt

Combine beef, onion, bay leaf, salt and pepper, and water. Cover and simmer 3 hours. Strain, bring to a boil, and add vegetables (except cabbage) and tomato puree. Cook 10 minutes. Add cabbage and cook until it is tender crisp. Top each bowl with a dollop of sour cream or yogurt into which pesto has been swirled.

33

PESTO GAZPACHO

Serves 6

3 tomatoes, peeled
1 green pepper, chopped
1 carrot, chopped
1 onion, chopped
¼ cup lemon juice
1 teaspoon lime juice
1 cucumber, peeled and chopped
3 sprigs of parsley
¼ cup pesto
3 cups chicken broth
Pine nuts

Blend half the ingredients, except pine nuts, in blender or food processor at high speed until smooth. Repeat with other half. Combine the two and chill well. Top with some pine nuts. Serve with Pesto Croutons. (See Index.)

EGG DISHES

PESTO FRITTATA

Serves 4–6

Frittata means "fried" in Italian. This dish brings out the real flavor of zucchini. Be sure to use tiny, tender ones.

4 small zucchini
4 tablespoons pesto
7 eggs
Salt

Cut zucchini into very thin rounds. Put pesto in heavy fry pan and cook zucchini in it until just wilted. Sprinkle with salt. Beat eggs and pour them over the zucchini. As soon as bottom is brown, slide spatula under one side, tilt the pan, and let more uncooked egg go to the bottom. When whole pan is almost solid, turn the frittata and finish cooking.

PESTO TUNA PIE

Serves 4–6

This is a simple and satisfying main dish.

1 unbaked 9-inch pie shell
1 large (12½-ounce can of tuna, drained)
1 cup shredded Swiss cheese
½ cup sliced green onion
3 eggs
½ cup mayonnaise
3 tablespoons pesto
½ cup whole milk (for a richer pie,
use evaporated milk)

Pierce pie shell with fork and bake at 375°F for 10 minutes. Remove from oven. In large bowl toss together next three ingredients. Spoon into pastry. In bowl stir together remaining ingredients. Slowly pour over tuna mixture. Bake 50 minutes at 350°F.

BROCCOLI SOUFFLÉ

Serves 4–6

This has a nice cheese flavor without a lot of cholesterol.

¼ cup butter
¼ cup flour
1 cup milk
1 tablespoon diced onion
½ cup mayonnaise
2 tablespoons pesto
3 eggs
2 10-ounce packages frozen chopped broccoli
(or 1 head fresh), cooked until not quite tender

Melt butter; add flour until it is a paste. Gradually add milk and cook until thickened. In a bowl mix together with a fork the onion, mayonnaise, pesto, and eggs. Add to white sauce and then add broccoli. Bake at 325°F for 35 minutes in buttered soufflé or loaf pan.

KENNEBUNKPORT SOUFFLÉ

Serves 6

8 slices white bread, trimmed and sliced
2 cups crabmeat
2 tablespoons mayonnaise
2 tablespoons pesto
1 onion, diced
1 green pepper, diced
2 cups milk
4 eggs, beaten
1½ cups cheddar cheese
Several handfuls of crushed potato chips

Preheat oven to 350°F. Place half of bread in a 12″ × 8″ × 2″ greased casserole dish. Mix all other ingredients (except potato chips) together and pour over bread. Place rest of bread on top with a sprinkle more of cheese. Top with potato chips. Bake for 1 hour.

GREEN EGGS AND HAM

Serves 6

2 pounds potatoes
3 tablespoons minced shallots
6 tablespoons butter
1 cup chopped ham
⅓ cup grated Parmesan cheese
6 eggs
Salt and pepper
1½ cups light cream
4 tablespoons pesto
2 tablespoons cognac

Peel, wash, and slice potatoes very thin. In a large skillet sauté potatoes and shallots in butter and cook until browned. Butter a casserole and spread the potatoes, shallots, and ham evenly over bottom. Sprinkle on cheese. Carefully break eggs, laying them on top of potato-ham mixture. Season with salt and pepper. Whisk pesto into cream and pour over eggs until just yolk shows. Dribble cognac over dish and bake 10 minutes at 375°F or until eggs are set.

PESTO QUICHE

Serves 4–6

I invented this recipe when I went to make the pastry in my food processor after having made a batch of pesto. I made the standard crust in the mixer without washing out the remaining bits of pesto.

SINGLE CRUST

1¼ cups flour
¼ cup vegetable shortening
½ teaspoon salt
1 tablespoon pesto
Cold water

Mix together all ingredients. Quickly add 3 tablespoons cold water. Pat dough into a ball, chill, and roll it out. Line a 9-inch pie pan with crust.

FILLING

1 cup grated Gruyère cheese
½ cup grated cheddar cheese
1 onion
1 green pepper
¼ pound mushrooms
4 tablespoons pesto
Sun-dried tomatoes
4 eggs
1¼ cups milk
3 tablespoons flour
Salt and pepper

Cover bottom of crust with cheeses. Gently sauté vegetables in pesto and add mixture to cheeses. Beat eggs with milk, flour, and several dashes of salt and pepper. Pour custard over vegetable layer. Top with some sun-dried tomatoes and bake at 350°F for 45 minutes.

PASTA
DISHES

TRADITIONAL PESTO WITH PASTA

Serves 4 (as main dish)
Serves 6 (as side dish)

Try this as a main dish or serve it on the side with Venison Cutlets or Lamb Kabobs. (See Index.) A great substitute for rice or potatoes, it also works well on a plate with dishes like Chicken Roman Style or Eggplant, where it can absorb some of the tomato sauce.

1 pound pasta
Grated Parmesan cheese
8 ounces pesto

Boil your favorite pasta until cooked al dente. Drain and place on a platter. Pour room temperature pesto over it. Toss with Parmesan cheese.

PESTO À LA GORGONZOLA

Serves 4

4 ounces Gorgonzola cheese
¼ cup heavy cream
8 ounces pesto
1 pound pasta, cooked and drained

In a heavy skillet over low heat mash Gorgonzola with cream and pesto. When smooth serve over pasta and toss.

PASTA WITH SHELLFISH AND PESTO

Serves 4

A sprig of opal basil nicely garnishes this dish.

2 tablespoons butter
1 pound scallops or shelled shrimp
8 ounces pesto
1 pound pasta

In a heavy skillet melt butter and sauté shellfish for 3–5 minutes. Stir in pesto and allow to simmer for 2 minutes. Toss with your favorite cooked, drained pasta and grated cheese.

FRANCIE'S RED PESTO CLAM SAUCE

Serves 6

I went to my sister-in law's for dinner, bringing along a nice bottle of Cabernet and a container of pesto. We had consumed most of the wine and were hungry but didn't really feel like spending much time preparing food. We inspected her cupboard and the resulting recipe was a huge success.

3 tablespoons pesto
1 teaspoon dried oregano
4 cups tomatoes, fresh or canned
¼ cup chopped fresh parsley
Dash of hot red pepper
12 pitted black olives, sliced
1 can anchovies or 2 tablespoons anchovy paste
3 10-ounce cans whole clams, reserve the juice
1 pound spaghetti
Black pepper

In a large skillet heat pesto and add oregano, tomatoes, parsley, and red pepper. Simmer uncovered for 30 minutes. Stir in olives, anchovies (or paste), and drained clams. Gently cook for 5 minutes, adding clam juice if sauce needs thinning. Serve over cooked drained pasta with freshly grated black pepper.

PESTO PASTA PRIMAVERA

Serves 6

This may seem like a long and involved recipe, but it goes quickly if you have your vegetables prepared and cooking utensils organized. It should be made at mealtime and served immediately. I like to sprinkle extra pine nuts and finely chopped fresh basil over the top.

1 bunch broccoli
2 small zucchini
4 asparagus spears
1½ cups green beans
½ cup peas
2 cups mushrooms
3 cups chopped tomatoes
4 ounces pesto
1 pound spaghetti
4 tablespoons butter
2 tablespoons chicken broth
½ cup heavy cream
⅔ cup grated Parmesan cheese

Chop and steam vegetables for 3–5 minutes until tender but still crisp. Drain and set aside. Cook tomatoes for 5 minutes in heavy skillet, stirring gently. Add pesto. Set aside.

In a large pot cook spaghetti until al dente. Drain in a colander and set aside.

In the same pasta pot melt butter, add broth, cream, and cheese. Stir constantly and cook gently until smooth. Add spaghetti, vegetables, and tomato-pesto sauce. Toss quickly with more grated cheese. Salt and pepper to taste.

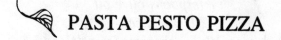 PASTA PESTO PIZZA

Serves 6

2 cups whole-grain macaroni (artichoke is nice)
2 eggs, beaten
½ cup chopped onion
¾ cup grated cheddar cheese
1½ cups tomato sauce
1 cup shredded mozzarella cheese
4 ounces pesto
1 cup sliced mushrooms
2 tablespoons chopped olives
1 green pepper, sliced

Cook macaroni until al dente. Add to eggs, onion, and cheddar cheese. Spread on a buttered cookie sheet. Bake at 375°F for 15 minutes. Spread with pesto, then tomato sauce. Top with remaining ingredients. Bake for 15 minutes more.

TORTELLINI WITH PESTO, VEGETABLES, AND FISH

Serves 4

8 ounces fresh salmon
8 ounces fresh swordfish
3 tablespoons olive oil
2 leeks, diced
8 ounces wild mushrooms (morels and
chanterelles are nice)
2 plum tomatoes, peeled and chopped
4 ounces pesto
1 pound cheese-filled tortellini, cooked and
drained
Freshly ground pepper

In a large heavy skillet sear the fish in 2
tablespoons oil for 3 minutes each side.
Remove, break into chunks, and set aside on a
plate. Pour 1 tablespoon oil in skillet and gently
sauté leeks and mushrooms for several minutes.
Add tomatoes, fish, and pesto. Slowly cook for
2 minutes more, stirring constantly. Add
tortellini. Toss with lots of pepper and serve.

PESTO COUSCOUS

One of my clients literally chased me down the beach (I was jogging) to tell me about this recipe discovery.

2 cups couscous
½ cup water
4 ounces pesto
1 cup each diced carrots, celery, green pepper,
red cabbage, broccoli, and fresh peas
3 cups chicken broth
1 cup button mushrooms
2 cups drained canned chick peas
Salt and pepper

Mix couscous and water together gently with fingers to moisten all grains. Cover and steam in couscous pot for 20 minutes. Stir and steam 20 minutes longer. Stir in half of the pesto. Meanwhile place all vegetables except mushrooms and chickpeas in a heavy saucepan. Add broth, cover, and cook about 10 minutes. Add mushrooms and chickpeas. Cook 5 minutes more. To serve, pile couscous in a deep dish in conical shape. Arrange drained vegetables around it. Swirl remaining pesto into remaining cup of cooking broth and pour over couscous.

MEAT,
FISH
&
VEGETABLES

PESTO STEAK

Serves 4

2 tablespoons olive oil
4 sirloin steaks
2 tablespoons pesto
2 tablespoons chopped shallots
¼ cup cognac
1½ cups heavy cream
1 tablespoon Dijon mustard
Salt and pepper

Heat oil in a large, very heavy skillet. When oil is hot, add steaks and cook on both sides until done. Remove steaks to a serving platter. Pour fat off from pan. Add pesto and shallots. Cook for 1 minute. Add cognac and ignite. Add cream and bring to a boil. Cook 5 minutes over high heat, stirring often. Remove from heat and stir in mustard. Salt and pepper to taste. Pour sauce over steak and serve.

BEEF STEW WITH PESTO

Serves 4

This goes well with lots of Pesto Bread.
(See Index.)

1 pound stew beef, cut in cubes
½ teaspoon each salt and pepper
4 tablespoons flour
3 tablespoons olive oil
1 12-ounce bottle dark beer
2 tablespoons dry red wine
3 carrots, chopped
1 large onion, chopped
3 medium potatoes, chopped
1 10-ounce package frozen peas
1 cup chopped mushrooms
4 tablespoons pesto
1 tablespoon Dijon mustard
1 tablespoon catsup
1 teaspoon dried thyme
1 tablespoon Worcestershire

Sprinkle salt and pepper (½ teaspoon each) on
stew beef and dredge with flour. Heat olive oil
in heavy pan and brown the meat in it. Add
beer and wine; cover. Simmer over low heat for
45 minutes. Add all the ingredients except
thyme, Worcestershire, and more salt and
pepper. Stir well and add enough water to cover
vegetables. Return to low heat, cover, and let
cook for 30 minutes more. Season with thyme,
Worcestershire, salt, and pepper.

PESTO BURGERS

Grill hamburgers until done. Mix together equal
parts of softened butter and Roquefort cheese.
Moisten mixture with a splash of cognac.
Spread this over tops of burgers. Then drizzle
them with pesto and serve in a bun with sliced
red onion.

PESTO HOT DOGS

This is a good suggestion for friends who have
never tried pesto because they don't like "hippie
food."

Pierce and boil hot dogs in beef boullion for 3
mintues. Drain. Spread them with pesto and roll
in grated cheddar cheese. Wrap each one with a
strip of bacon. Place on a pan in broiler and
grill until bacon crisps. Serve on a toasted bun
with lots of whole-grain mustard and sliced
fresh tomato.

PESTO MEAT LOAF

Serves 4

Put some potatoes in the oven while this is cooking. "Pestocize" them (see Index for the Besto Potato) and serve with this meat loaf and a big salad.

1 egg
½ cup tomato sauce
1 tablespoon Dijon mustard
1 teaspoon Worcestershire
½ teaspoon dried thyme
1 onion, chopped fine
1 clove garlic, crushed
3 tablespoons pesto
¾ cup Italian bread crumbs
½ teaspoon each salt and pepper
1 pound very lean ground round
½ cup pine nuts (if available)
1 teaspoon dried oregano

In a large bowl, beat egg and add all ingredients except ground round, pine nuts, and oregano. When well blended, add ground round and mix thoroughly. Press mixture evenly into a loaf pan. Cover top with oregano and a sprinkling of pine nuts. Bake for 1 hour at 350°F.

PESTO LIVER

Serves 4

3 tablespoons butter
3 tablespoons pesto
2 spanish onions, sliced very thin
3 tablespoons chopped parsley
½ teaspoon salt
2 pounds calves liver, sliced no thicker
than ¼ inch

Heat butter and pesto over medium heat in a big frying pan. Add onions and sauté until translucent. Add salt and liver to onions and sauté quickly—2 minutes per side. Add parsley, stir, and cook 1 minute more.

OYSTERS AND SWEETBREADS ON SKEWERS À LA PESTO

Oysters
Sweetbreads
Bacon

Toss large oysters in pesto and wrap in strips of bacon secured with a toothpick. Alternate wrapped oysters on skewers with pieces of sweetbreads that have been first boiled for 20 minutes and then tossed in pesto. Cook over coals or under broiler, turning frequently until bacon is crisp.

TUNA LOIN "AU POIVRE AND PESTO" WITH TOMATO-PESTO RELISH

Serves 2

8 ounces tuna fish loin
Salt and cayenne pepper to taste
1 cup olive oil
1 tablespoon pesto
1½ cups cracked black pepper

Clean tuna fish loin, (skin off) and season with salt and cayenne. Combine ½ cup oil with pesto. Dip tuna into this and then roll it in the cracked black pepper, making sure to cover it all. Heat the rest of the olive oil (½ cup) in a heavy pan and sauté the tuna fish 30 seconds on each side or until medium rare (pink inside). Remove and keep warm.

TOMATO-PESTO RELISH

3 fresh plum tomatoes
1 branch fresh thyme
Salt and pepper to taste
2 fresh shallots, chopped
⅓ cup pesto

Plunge the tomatoes in boiling water for 1
minute, then plunge them into ice water for a
few seconds. Peel the tomatoes, cut in half, and
squeeze out the seeds and juice. Chop tomatoes
concasse style (in chunks). Heat pesto in heavy
pan and add chopped tomatoes and shallots.
Cook for 2 minutes. Salt and pepper to taste.
Keep warm. To serve, put relish on bottom of
plate. Slice the tuna and place on top of relish.
Garnish with fresh basil leaves.

PESTO VENISON CUTLETS

This also works nicely with pork or veal cutlets.

Venison cutlets
Fresh lemon juice
Bread crumbs
Olive oil

Spread cutlets generously with pesto. Squeeze a little fresh lemon juice over the tops and roll them in bread crumbs. Heat olive oil in skillet. Sauté cutlets until both sides are brown and meat is cooked through (about 5 minutes on each side, depending on thickness of cutlet).

PESTO LAMB KABOBS

Cut into bite-size chunks:

Fresh lamb meat
Green peppers
Onions
Zucchini
Fresh tomatoes
Mushrooms

Salt lightly and toss with pesto. Place ingredients alternately on skewers and roast over hot coals.

PESTO ROAST LAMB WITH ORZO

Serves 4

1 5–6 pound leg of lamb
Salt and pepper
1 cup thinly sliced onion
4 tablespoons pesto
4 cups canned plum tomatoes
½ cup water or dry red wine
5 cups beef broth
2 cups orzo
Grated Parmesan cheese

Preheat oven to 400°F. Rub lamb with salt and pepper. Place in shallow 12″ × 15″ roasting pan. Scatter onion around roast and pour pesto over meat. Bake 20 minutes until brown. Lower temperature to 350°F. Add tomatoes and water or wine. Cook about 1½ hours. Baste several times. Remove the lamb to a platter. Add broth and orzo to roasting pan. Stir and continue to bake for 20 minutes. Sprinkle with grated Parmesan cheese and serve with carved lamb.

SWORDFISH, SALMON, OR STEAK OVER COALS

This is a good use of pesto for a backpacking trip. Freeze thick sections of fish or meat and a container of pesto ahead of time. By the time you've reached your campsite the foods will be thawed. Simply baste fish or meat with pesto and cook over coals. It's also a nice idea for a backyard or beach barbecue.

If you want to cook the meat or fish in a broiler, first sprinkle a little lemon juice and white wine over the fish or soy sauce and red wine over the meat. Then baste it with pesto and cook until done. The juices in the broiler pan make a wonderful sauce over potatoes or rice.

 # PESTO FROG LEGS

Serves 2

4 frog legs
Flour
Salt and pepper
¼ cup butter
½ cup chicken stock
¼ cup pesto
¾ cup bread crumbs
1 teaspoon lemon juice

Clean legs and roll them in flour. Season with
salt and pepper. Melt butter in a skillet. Brown
legs in butter. Reduce heat and add stock.
Cover skillet and cook legs until tender. Mix
together pesto, bread crumbs, and lemon juice.
Roll legs in crumb mixture and brown lightly
under broiler.

PESTO SMOTHERED RABBIT

Serves 2–3

1 rabbit
Salt and pepper
Flour
2 tablespoons bacon drippings
2 onions, sliced
1 cup sour cream
3 tablespoons pesto
½ cup red wine
Splash of cognac

Clean and cut rabbit. Season with salt and
pepper. Dredge it with flour. Melt bacon
drippings in a pot. Sauté rabbit in drippings
until browned. Cover with onions and several
dashes of salt. Combine sour cream and pesto.
Pour over onions along with the wine and
cognac. Cover pot and simmer for 1 hour or
bake in a slow oven (325°F) for 1 hour.

ITALIAN SAUSAGES WITH PESTO

Serves 2–3

This dish is nice served with plenty of pesto bread.

¾ pound sweet Italian sausage
2 tablespoons pesto
1 onion, sliced thin
2 red peppers, cut in strips
2 large tomatoes, chopped
Freshly ground pepper

In a fry pan cook sausages until well browned. Remove sausages and pour off fat. Put pesto in pan and gently cook onion in it until soft. Add red pepper strips and cook 2 minutes more. Add tomatoes, sausages, and black pepper. Stir and cook over medium heat 2 minutes. Cover and simmer 20 minutes.

PESTO SQUID

Serves 4

1–3 pound package frozen squid,
if fresh is not available
4 tablespoons pesto
2 tablespoons fresh, finely chopped parsley
2 teaspoons salt
1 cup dry red wine
3 cups peeled plum tomatoes
1½ 10-ounce packages frozen peas
(or 3 cups fresh)

Clean squid and cut into pieces. Heat pesto in a big fry pan and add squid, parsley, and salt. After 3 minutes pour in wine and cook 3 more minutes. Add tomatoes, mashing them with a wooden spoon. Simmer for about 15 minutes. Add peas and cook for 15 minutes more.

PESTO CHICKEN

Serves 4

2 whole boneless, skinless chicken breasts,
halved
Salt and pepper
1 tablespoon olive oil
2 tablespoons pesto
4 ounces mozzarella cheese, cut into
⅛-inch-thick slices
1 cup mushrooms

Place chicken breasts between sheets of waxed paper. Pound to ½-inch thickness. Sprinkle with salt and pepper. In a large skillet heat olive oil and brown chicken lightly. Remove from heat. Spread 1 tablespoon pesto over the top of each breast. Cover with cheese. Return to pan and add mushrooms around sides. Cover and cook over low heat for 4 minutes.

CHICKEN ROMAN STYLE WITH PESTO

Serves 4 (generously)

This is a traditional Roman dish for celebrating the Feast of the Assumption, August 15. Roasting the peppers first gives them a wonderfully earthy taste which is definitely worth the effort.

3 sweet red and 3 green peppers
(or 6 of either kind)
4 tablespoons olive oil
8 parts frying chicken (I suggest 4 legs and
2 whole split breasts)
4 tablespoons pesto
4 cups peeled plum tomatoes
2 teaspoons salt
1 teaspoon pepper

Roast peppers accordingly. *On top of gas stove* roast whole peppers over flame holding them with a long wooden handled fork. *In an electric stove*, they can be roasted in the broiler as close to the heating element as possible. If you are having dinner by firelight, they can be roasted *over the open fire* in true Roman style. Whatever manner you choose, be sure to roast each side until completely charred. Then put them under running cold water and peel off black skin. Slice peppers into half-inch-wide strips, discarding stem and seeds.

Put olive oil in large, heavy pan over medium heat. Add chicken and fry on both sides until golden brown. Remove pieces and set aside to drain. Pour all the oil out of the pan and discard. Put pesto in the pan over medium heat and add tomatoes, crushing them with a wooden spoon. Bring to a boil. Add half the pepper strips, chicken, salt, and pepper. Cook for 20 minutes, uncovered. Add the remaining pepper strips and cook for one minute more.

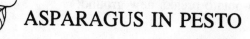 ## ASPARAGUS IN PESTO

Serves 4–6

2 pounds asparagus
4 ounces pesto
½ cup grated Parmesan cheese
¼ pound prosciutto

Cook asparagus until tender yet still firm. Drain and wrap each spear in very thinly sliced prosciutto. Arrange in single layer in buttered baking dish. Pour pesto over top and sprinkle with cheese. Bake in 400°F oven for 10 minutes.

PESTO GOES TO THE COUNTY
(or "The Besto Potato")

In Maine potatoes are mostly raised in Aroostook County—a northernmost section that is referred to as simply "The County." It was settled several hundred years ago by Swedish immigrants. When I went there to visit a friend of Swedish descent I brought her some pesto. She had never heard of it, so we decided to try it with a familiar food. The result was delicious and my friend is now a pesto convert. The pesto-potato breaks new ground!

Baking potatoes
Sour cream
Pesto
Butter
Salt and pepper
Grated cheese

Bake potatoes until done. Cut them in half and scoop out. For each potato use 1 tablespoon sour cream, 1 teaspoon pesto, 1 teaspoon butter, and salt and pepper to taste. Mash well with a fork and put this stuffing back into potato skins. Sprinkle grated cheese (use your own personal favorite) over the tops and put potatoes back in the hot oven for 10 minutes.

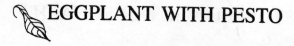 EGGPLANT WITH PESTO

Serves 8

2 large eggplant
2 eggs, beaten
2 cups bread crumbs
8 ounces pesto
1 quart tomato sauce
1 pound Mozzarella cheese, grated
Olive oil

Slice eggplant ½-inch thick. Dip pieces first into egg, then bread crumbs. Fry in oil on each side until tender and brown. In greased 9″ × 13″ pan layer eggplant with pesto, tomato sauce, and cheese. Bake 20 minutes covered at 350°F. Uncover and bake 10 minutes more.

STUFFED WINTER SQUASH

Serves 6

This is a nice change from the traditional method of preparing winter squash (with syrup, cinnamon, etc.).

6 small or 3 large butternut or acorn squash
6 slices of bacon
½ cup chopped onion
8 ounces pesto
½ teaspoon each salt and pepper
½ cup sauterne

Split squash and scoop out centers, discarding pith and seeds. Chop squash flesh. In a skillet fry bacon until crisp. Drain and crumble it. Pour off all but 2 tablespoons fat and in this sauté onion until soft. Add squash flesh and cook for 3 minutes. Mix in bacon, salt, and pepper and spoon this stuffing back into shells. Arrange in shallow greased baking pan. Spoon pesto over tops. Pour wine over squash. Cover pan with aluminum foil and bake at 350°F for 30 minutes. Remove foil for last 5 minutes.

SALADS,

DRESSINGS

&

SAUCES

PESTO POTATO SALAD

Serves 6–8

*6 large potatoes, peeled, diced, cooked, and
drained
3 hard boiled eggs, peeled and chopped
1 cup chopped celery
4 ounces pitted black olives, chopped
1 cup mayonnaise
4 ounces pesto
2 tablespoons mustard
Salt and pepper
3 slices cooked bacon, crumbled
1 red onion, sliced thin*

Mix potatoes, eggs, celery, and olives in a
bowl. Combine mayonnaise, pesto, and
mustard. Toss with ingredients in bowl. Salt
and pepper to taste. Top with bacon and onion.

PESTO BULGAR SALAD

Serves 6–8

2¾ cups boiling chicken broth
1½ cups raw bulgar
4 ounces pesto
2 tablespoons lemon juice
1 tablespoon lime juice
1 cucumber, chopped
1 green pepper, chopped
1 carrot, chopped
Salt and pepper

Pour broth over bulgar in large bowl. Cover and let sit for 30 minutes. Combine pesto with juices and add to the bulgar. Toss in vegetables and season to taste. Chill and garnish with mint leaves. This salad goes nicely with pesto biscuits. (See Index.)

PESTO DOWN ON THE BAYOU

Serves 4–6

My daughter came home from New Orleans last Christmas with this recipe idea—a nice winter salad.

1 cup cooked wheat berries
1 cup cooked brown rice
4 ounces cut up cheddar cheese
4 ounces walnut meats
1 tomato, chopped
1 teaspoon sweet paprika
4 ounces pesto
1 tablespoon cumin
1 teaspoon chili powder
Salt and pepper

Combine all ingredients in a bowl. Salt and pepper to taste.

PESTO VEGETABLE SALAD

Steam wax beans, shelled peas, and baby
carrots in a steamer for 3 minutes. Add thinly
sliced zucchini and steam for 1 minute more.
Drain vegetables and place in a bowl. Toss with
pesto and slivered almonds. Salt and pepper to
taste and garnish with fresh parsley. May be
served warm or chilled. Nice with Pesto
Popovers.

 # SPINACH SALAD

Combine fresh spinach leaves, sliced
mushrooms, and cubes of feta cheese in a bowl.
Toss with pesto and garnish with extra pine
nuts.

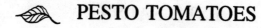 # PESTO TOMATOES

This is also wonderful without the vinegar.

3 large ripe tomatoes, sliced
4 ounces pesto
1 tablespoon red wine vinegar
Black olives
Fresh basil leaves
Crusty Italian bread

Arrange tomato slices on a platter. Combine pesto and vinegar and pour over tomatoes. Garnish with olives and leaves. Serve with the bread.

PESTO SALSA

Makes 2 cups

1 cup diced peeled tomatoes
½ cup tomato juice
3 scallions, chopped
½ cup diced green or red pepper
½ teaspoon chili powder
1 tablespoon lime juice
2 tablespoons pesto
1 jalapeno pepper
½ teaspoon hot paprika

Mix ingredients together until well blended. Salt and pepper to taste. Serve with tacos and tortillas.

PESTO ARTICHOKE DIP

Makes enough dip for 1 large artichoke

2 tablespoons melted butter
2 tablespoons pesto
1 teaspoon lemon juice
1 teaspoon grated Parmesan cheese

Mix together with freshly ground pepper. Serve with cooked artichokes.

84

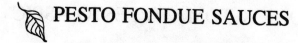# PESTO FONDUE SAUCES

Each sauce serves 2

BEEF FONDUE

Mix together:

6 ounces tomato paste
1 teaspoon dry mustard
1 teaspoon horseradish
1 tablespoon pesto

SCALLOP FONDUE

Mix together:

1 tablespoon pesto
1 teaspoon lemon juice
4 tablespoons mayonnaise

Roll scallops in bread crumbs before cooking.

QUICK TOMATO PESTO ASPIC

Serves 6

2 tablespoons unflavored gelatin
½ cup cold tomato juice
3½ cups hot tomato juice
2 tablespoons pesto
Dash of Worcestershire
1 cup of combination of chopped celery, olives,
green pepper, and carrots
½ cup mayonnaise
1 tablespoon pesto
1 tablespoon horseradish

Soak gelatin in cold tomato juice, then dissolve mixture in hot juice. Stir in 2 tablespoons pesto and the Worcestershire. Chill aspic in a mold. When it is about to set, add vegetables. Chill until firm and serve with a dressing made of mayonnaise, pesto, and horseradish.

PESTO SALAD DRESSING I

This tastes great on a "Winter Salad" that might include chopped red cabbage, carrots, and onion with chunks of cheddar cheese and a sprinkle of sunflower seeds.

10 shelled walnuts
1 teaspoon dry mustard
½ teaspoon cayenne
1 tablespoon minced chives
1 cup pesto
¼ cup red wine vinegar
¼ cup dry red wine
¼ teaspoon salt

Blend all ingredients in a blender.

PESTO SALAD DRESSING II

This is wonderful on a more traditional tossed salad. The dressing coats leaves of Boston lettuce nicely. Be sure to include chopped ripe tomatoes and thinly sliced crisp cucumber.

1 cup olive oil
2 tablespoons tahini
2 tablespoons lemon juice
2 tablespoons pesto
1 tablespoon red wine vinegar
1 teaspoon Dijon mustard or
whole-grain mustard
½ teaspoon salt

Combine all ingredients in a jar and shake until well blended.

BAKED GOODS,

BREADS

&

SANDWICHES

PESTO BREAD

You'll never make plain garlic bread again.

Slice a loaf of French or Italian bread
lengthwise. Spread cut sides with lots of pesto.
Sprinkle with grated Parmesan or Romano
cheese and heat in oven 10 minutes.

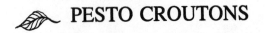 # PESTO CROUTONS

Dice stale bread into cubes. Toss with pesto and
freshly grated black pepper. Roast in a 375°F
oven, turning occasionally until crisp. Let sit on
paper towels before serving or storing in airtight
container.

PESTO BISCUITS

These go nicely with a salad for lunch. For a heartier meal, serve with the Soupe de Poisson and Pesto. (See Index.)

2 cups flour
3 teaspoons baking powder
1 teaspoon salt
¼ cup cold butter
½ cup grated cheddar cheese
2 tablespoons pesto
¾ cup cold milk
Margarine or bacon fat

Sift flour, baking powder, and salt. Cut in butter, cheese, and pesto. Add milk quickly. Grease muffin tins with margarine or fat. Fill ⅔ full. Bake for 12 minutes at 425°F. Makes 12.

PESTO POPOVERS

If you use smoked cheese, these are particularly good for breakfast. They have a bacon flavor but none of the saturated fat content. They also taste wonderful with no cheese at all.

Spread pans with margarine and heat for 10 minutes in a 425°F oven.

1 cup flour
2 eggs
⅓ cup grated cheddar cheese
(smoked if available)
⅞ cup milk
1 tablespoon pesto

Mix together in blender all ingredients except the cheese. Fill individual pans ⅓ full with batter. Place 1 heaping teaspoon cheese on top of each one. Cover with batter until ⅔ full. Bake for 25 minutes at 425°F. Serve immediately. Makes 6 large popovers.

SANDWICHES

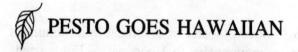 THE BESTO PESTO

Grill thick slices of Italian bread in olive oil and spread with pesto. Fill with sliced Swiss cheese, avocado, and red onion. Heat in oven until cheese melts.

PESTO GOES HAWAIIAN

In a fry pan fry a ½-inch-thick slice of Gruyère cheese until soft. Top with a slice of fresh pineapple and place between slices of toasted pumpernickel bread that have been spread with pesto.

THE PESTO POCKET

Sauté ½ cup of chopped onion and 2½ cups minced eggplant in 1 tablespoon olive oil. Salt and remove from heat. Toss with 2 tablespoons pesto and ½ cup chopped black olives. Fill halves of pita bread with this mixture and top with a sprinkle of shredded mozzarella cheese. Heat until cheese melts.

THE POWER PACK

Spread softened cream cheese on slices of
whole-grain bread. Fill with sliced ham,
cucumbers, several dollops of pesto, and
sprouts.

LOBSTER OR CRABMEAT
ROLLS SUPREME

Toss cooked lobster or crabmeat in a mixture of
2 parts mayonnaise to 1 part pesto. Fill toasted
rolls with this mixture. If using lobster, squeeze
a little fresh lemon juice over the top and
garnish with parsley. If using crabmeat, grate a
little Swiss cheese over the top. Heat quickly
until cheese melts.

94

PESTO PIZZA

Serves 4–6

CRUST

1 package dry yeast
1 cup warm water
2 tablespoons olive oil
Dash of salt
1 teaspoon honey
2½ cups flour
1 teaspoon crushed fresh garlic
Pesto

Dissolve yeast in water. Stir in oil, honey, and garlic. Let sit 5 minutes. Add flour and salt. Knead, adding flour to keep dough from getting sticky. Spread onto greased cookie sheet and bake at 450°F for 5 minutes. Spread with lots of pesto (at least 4 ounces).

TOPPING

Tomato sauce or sliced tomatoes
Grated provolone cheese
Chopped olives
Diced mushrooms, green pepper, and onions

Or if you are pressed for time, order out for your favorite pizza and drizzle lots of pesto over the top. Quickly reheat in the oven.

PESTO PASTIES

Makes 6 hearty pasties

The original recipe was brought to Northern Michigan by Welsh miners. They carried these hot "turnovers" against their bodies into the mines to keep the midday meal warm. When visiting relatives in Wisconsin, my cousin offered to prepare pasties and I offered to "pestocize" them with some fresh pesto I had brought along on the plane. It was a great match. Those miners never knew what they were missing!

CRUST

⅓ pound lard
3 cups flour
1 teaspoon sugar
1 teaspoon salt
1 cup water

Cut lard into flour and mix together quickly with the rest of the ingredients. Chill and form into 6 balls.

FILLING

½ pound pork steak
1 pound sirloin or round steak
1 large onion
Salt and pepper
3 potatoes
1 rutabaga and 1 eggplant, all peeled and diced
6 tablespoons pesto

Cut meat and onion into chunks. Place in large bowl. Toss with salt and pepper and let sit while dough is chilling. Add vegetables to meat mixture and toss with the pesto. Roll dough balls out into circles, flouring the board if necessary. Place filling on half of the circle, fold over and pinch to seal edges. Prick the tops and bake for 1 hour at 375°F. Serve with catsup for real midwestern eating.

A GREEK 'PESTOED' PASTRY

FILO WITH PESTO

Serves 8

Serve with Spinach Salad, leaving out the feta cheese, or with Potage St. Germaine. (See Index.)

FILLING

½ cup finely chopped onion
½ cup finely chopped mushrooms
2 tablespoons butter
2 cups crumbled feta cheese
2 tablespoons flour
1 pound cottage cheese
3 tablespoons pesto
5 eggs, lightly beaten

You'll also need

1 pound package of defrosted filo dough
½ pound melted butter
½ cup pine nuts

Cook onions and mushrooms in the 2
tablespoons butter until soft. Mix together with
all ingredients excepts filo, melted butter, and
pine nuts.

Spread a little melted butter in a 9″ × 13″
baking pan. Spread a filo leaf in the bottom of
the pan, letting edges go up the sides. Brush
with butter. Repeat the process until you have
about 8 layers of dough. Spread on ½ of the
filling. Keep layering dough with melted butter
8 more times. Spread the rest of the filling. Add
8 more layers of filo (buttering between each
one). Butter the top leaf and sprinkle with pine
nuts. Fold over corners of dough. Bake
uncovered for 40 minutes at 375°F.

PESTOVERS

(THE REVIVAL OF LEFTOVERS THROUGH PESTO)

THREE PESTO REBIRTHS

TUNA NOODLE CASSEROLE
LASAGNE
CHICKEN POT PIE

These frequently served dishes are often found, several days later, unwanted and dried out in the refrigerator. A generous application of pesto over the top before covering and heating will give them new life.

PESTO CORN

Spread leftover cooked ears of corn generously with a mixture of half pesto and half melted butter. Roll in Parmesan cheese and freshly ground pepper. Wrap in foil and heat for 10 minutes in a 400°F oven.

VEGETABLE RICE CASSEROLE

Serves 4

I can often use up leftover cooked rice and vegetables this way.

1 cup cooked rice
2 eggs, lightly beaten
1 pound cottage cheese
2 cups cooked vegetables
Grated Parmesan cheese
1 onion, chopped
Salt and pepper
4 ounces pesto

Combine all ingredients. Cover and bake for 30 minutes at 350°F.

WHAT`S

FOR

DESSERT?

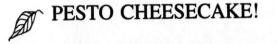# PESTO CHEESECAKE!

Serves 12 (cut each quarter section into thirds)

When I dream of Italy, I remember smells that seem to be a combination of espresso, sweetness, garlic, and cooked dough. This cake sums it all up. I know some garlic aficionadas who say that they love garlic in everything except chocolate. I can now say that I love pesto in everything—including chocolate!

CRUST

¾ stick butter
¼ cup sugar
1 egg
1¼ cups flour
1 teaspoon baking powder

Melt butter in saucepan. Whisk in remaining ingredients until well blended. Press into a 9-inch springform or deep-dish pie pan. Work with fingers to form 1-inch-high sides. Chill while making the filling.

FILLING

5 squares melted semi-sweet chocolate
(or 5 ounces chips)
16 ounces cream cheese
⅓ cup sugar
½ cup freshly brewed espresso (or ½ cup
regular coffee, made double-strength)
2 eggs
1 cup milk
1 teaspoon pesto

Blend all ingredients in a blender or food
processor. Pour into prepared crust and bake for
45 minutes at 350°F. Allow to cool in oven.
Serve at room temperature or chilled.

INDEX

109